Quotable Wilde

QUOTABLE WILDE

Summersdale Publishers Ltd
46 West Street
Chichester
West Sussex
PO19 1RP
UK

www.summersdale.com

Printed and bound in the Czech Republic

ISBN: 978-1-84953-695-0

Substantial discounts on bulk quantities of Summersdale books are available to corporations, professional associations and other organisations. For details contact Nicky Douglas by telephone: +44 (0) 1243 756902, fax: +44 (0) 1243 786300 or email: nicky@summersdale.com.

Quotable Wilde

summersdale

Contents

Mankind and Morality

*I can resist everything
except temptation.*

Lord Darlington, *Lady Windermere's Fan*

*A thing is not
necessarily true because
a man dies for it.*

Erskine, *The Portrait of Mr W. H.*

The truth is rarely pure and never simple. Modern life would be very tedious if it were either, and modern literature a complete impossibility.

Algernon, *The Importance of Being Earnest*

Ambition is the last refuge of the failure.

Phrases and Philosophies for the Use of the Young

The one duty we owe to history is to rewrite it.

Gilbert, *The Critic as Artist*

*Life is much too
important a thing ever to
talk seriously about it.*

Prince Paul, *Vera; or, the Nihilists*

Sometimes the poor are praised for being thrifty. But to recommend thrift to the poor is both grotesque and insulting. It is like advising a man who is starving to eat less.

The Soul of Man Under Socialism

People are very fond of giving away what they need most themselves. It is what I call the depth of generosity.

Lord Henry, *The Picture of Dorian Gray*

It is always a silly thing to give advice, but to give good advice is absolutely fatal.

Erskine, *The Portrait of Mr W. H.*

The things people say of a man do not alter a man. He is what he is. Public opinion is of no value whatsoever.

The Soul of Man Under Socialism

*Only the shallow
know themselves.*

Phrases and Philosophies for the Use of the Young

*Nowadays most people
die of a sort of creeping
common sense, and discover
when it is too late that
the only things one never
regrets are one's mistakes.*

Lord Henry, *The Picture of Dorian Gray*

One can survive everything
nowadays, except death.

Lord Illingworth, *A Woman of No Importance*

To make a good salad is to be a brilliant diplomatist – the problem is so entirely the same in both cases. To know exactly how much oil one must put with one's vinegar.

Prince Paul, *Vera; or, the Nihilists*

I tell you that there are terrible temptations that it requires strength, strength and courage, to yield to.

Sir Robert Chiltern, *An Ideal Husband*

I can stand brute force, but brute reason is quite unbearable. There is something unfair about its use. It is hitting below the intellect.

Lord Henry, *The Picture of Dorian Gray*

As long as war is regarded
as wicked, it will always
have its fascination. When
it is looked upon as vulgar,
it will cease to be popular.

Gilbert, *The Critic as Artist*

*The only difference
between the saint and
the sinner is that every
saint has a past, and every
sinner has a future.*

Lord Illingworth, *A Woman of No Importance*

If one tells the truth,
one is sure, sooner or
later, to be found out.

Phrases and Philosophies for the Use of the Young

High hopes were once formed of democracy; but democracy means simply the bludgeoning of the people by the people for the people.

The Soul of Man Under Socialism

*There is no sin
except stupidity.*

Gilbert, *The Critic as Artist*

The only way to get rid of a temptation is to yield to it.

Lord Henry, *The Picture of Dorian Gray*

My experience is that as soon as people are old enough to know better, they don't know anything at all.

Cecil Graham, *Lady Windermere's Fan*

Conscience and cowardice are really the same things... Conscience is the trade name of the firm. That is all.

Lord Henry, *The Picture of Dorian Gray*

Selfishness is not living as one wishes to live, it is asking others to live as one wishes to live.

The Soul of Man Under Socialism

*Patriotism is the
vice of nations.*

Phrases and Philosophies for the Use of the Young

What a pity that in life we only get our lessons when they are of no use to us.

Lady Windermere, *Lady Windermere's Fan*

In examinations the foolish ask questions that the wise cannot answer.

Phrases and Philosophies for the Use of the Young

It is only the intellectually lost who ever argue.

Lord Henry, *The Picture of Dorian Gray*

Foolish Hearts

Men marry because they are tired; women, because they are curious: both are disappointed.

Lord Henry, *The Picture of Dorian Gray*

The only way to behave to a woman is to make love to her if she is pretty and to someone else if she is plain.

Algernon, *The Importance of Being Earnest*

All sins, except a
sin against itself, Love
should forgive.

Sir Robert Chiltern, *An Ideal Husband*

*An engagement should come
on a young girl as a surprise,
pleasant or unpleasant
as the case may be.*

Lady Bracknell, *The Importance of Being Earnest*

*The one charm of marriage
is that it makes a life
of deception absolutely
necessary for both parties.*

Lord Henry, *The Picture of Dorian Gray*

*To love oneself is
the beginning of a
lifelong romance.*

Lord Goring, *An Ideal Husband*

When a woman marries again,
it is because she detested her
first husband. When a man
marries again, it is because he
adored his first wife. Women
try their luck; men risk theirs.

Lord Henry, *The Picture of Dorian Gray*

Those who are faithful know only the trivial side of love; it is the faithless who know love's tragedies.

Lord Henry, *The Picture of Dorian Gray*

The very essence of romance is uncertainty.

Algernon, *The Importance of Being Earnest*

A grande passion *is the
privilege of people who
have nothing to do.*

Lord Henry, *The Picture of Dorian Gray*

In married life three is company, and two is none.

Algernon, *The Importance of Being Earnest*

When one is in love, one always begins by deceiving one's self, and one always ends by deceiving others. That is what the world calls a romance.

Lord Henry, *The Picture of Dorian Gray*

The people who love only once in their lives are really the shallow people. What they call their loyalty, and their fidelity, I call either the lethargy of custom or their lack of imagination.

Lord Henry, *The Picture of Dorian Gray*

Keep love in your heart. A life without it is like a sunless garden when the flowers are dead. The consciousness of loving and being loved brings warmth and richness to life that nothing else can bring.

I have always been of opinion that a man who desires to get married should know either everything or nothing.

Lady Bracknell, *The Importance of Being Earnest*

*The mystery of love
is greater than the
mystery of death.*

Salome, Salome

To be in love is to surpass one's self.

Sibyl Vane, *The Picture of Dorian Gray*

The Truth of Men and Women

Women love us for
our defects. If we have
enough of them, they will
forgive us everything,
even our intellects.

Lord Henry, *The Picture of Dorian Gray*

One is tempted to define man
as a rational animal who always
loses his temper when he is
called upon to act in accordance
with the dictates of reason.

Gilbert, *The Critic as Artist*

*Friendship is far
more tragic than love.
It lasts longer.*

A Few Maxims for the Instruction of the Over-Educated

Between men and women there is no friendship possible. There is passion, enmity, worship, love, but no friendship.

Lord Darlington, *Lady Windermere's Fan*

The growing influence of women is the one reassuring thing in our political life.

Kelvil, *A Woman of No Importance*

Women represent the
triumph of matter
over mind, just as men
represent the triumph
of mind over morals.

Lord Henry, *The Picture of Dorian Gray*

Women have a wonderful instinct about things. They can discover everything except the obvious.

Lord Goring, *An Ideal Husband*

Thirty-five is a very attractive age. London society is full of women of the very highest birth who have, of their own free choice, remained thirty-five for years.

Lady Bracknell, *The Importance of Being Earnest*

Lord Caversham: *No woman, plain or pretty, has any common sense at all, sir. Common sense is the privilege of our sex.*
Lord Goring: *Quite so. And we men are so self-sacrificing that we never use it, do we, father?*

An Ideal Husband

An excellent man: he has no enemies, and none of his friends like him.

On George Bernard Shaw

Experience, the name men give to their mistakes.

Prince Paul, *Vera; or, the Nihilists*

*If a man is a gentleman,
he knows quite enough,
and if he is not a
gentleman, whatever he
knows is bad for him.*

Lord Fermor, *The Picture of Dorian Gray*

*Women are never
disarmed by compliments.
Men always are.*

Mrs Cheveley, An Ideal Husband

Man is least himself when he talks in his own person. Give him a mask, and he will tell you the truth.

Gilbert, *The Critic as Artist*

*It is absurd to divide
people into good and
bad. People are either
charming or tedious.*

Lord Darlington, *Lady Windermere's Fan*

Lord Goring: *Now I'm going to give you some good advice.*
Mrs Cheveley: *Pray don't. You should never give a woman anything that she can't wear in the evening.*

An Ideal Husband

Lord Illingworth: *The Book of Life begins with a man and a woman in a garden. Mrs Allonby: It ends with Revelations.*

A Woman of No Importance

[Women] spoil every romance by trying to make it last for ever.

Lord Henry, *The Picture of Dorian Gray*

Cecil Graham:
What is a cynic?
Lord Darlington: *A man who knows the price of everything and the value of nothing.*

Lady Windermere's Fan

If we men married the women we deserved, we should have a very bad time of it.

Lord Goring, *An Ideal Husband*

The mere fact of having published a book of second-rate sonnets makes a man quite irresistible. He lives the poetry that he cannot write.

Lord Henry, *The Picture of Dorian Gray*

A Fine Life

*We are all in the gutter,
but some of us are
looking at the stars.*

Lord Darlington, *Lady Windermere's Fan*

I like persons better than principles, and I like persons with no principles better than anything else in the world.

Lord Henry, *The Picture of Dorian Gray*

There is only one class in the community that thinks more about money than the rich, and that is the poor.

The Soul of Man Under Socialism

*I have the simplest
tastes. I am always
satisfied with the best.*

Lord Illingworth, *A Woman of No Importance*

*Education is an admirable
thing. But it is well to
remember from time to time
that nothing that is worth
knowing can be taught.*

A Few Maxims for the Instruction of the Over-Educated

There are few things easier than to live badly and to die well.

Prince Paul, *Vera; or, the Nihilists*

I never travel without my diary. One should always have something sensational to read in the train.

Gwendolen, *The Importance of Being Earnest*

It is always nice to be expected, and not to arrive.

Lord Goring, *An Ideal Husband*

*Indifference is the
revenge the world takes
on mediocrities.*

Prince Paul, *Vera; or, the Nihilists*

Laughter is not at all a bad beginning for a friendship, and it is far the best ending for one.

Lord Henry, *The Picture of Dorian Gray*

One should always be
a little improbable.

Phrases and Philosophies for the Use of the Young

Nowadays we are all of us so hard up that the only pleasant things to pay are compliments.

Lord Darlington, *Lady Windermere's Fan*

The English country gentleman galloping after a fox – the unspeakable in full pursuit of the uneatable.

Lord Illingworth, *A Woman of No Importance*

Moderation is a fatal thing... Nothing succeeds like excess.

Lord Illingworth, *A Woman of No Importance*

No gentleman ever has any money.

Algernon, *The Importance of Being Earnest*

If it took Labouchere three columns to prove that I was forgotten, then there is no difference between fame and obscurity.

*Most modern calendars
mar the sweet simplicity of
our lives by reminding us
that each day that passes
is the anniversary of some
perfectly uninteresting event.*

'A New Calendar'

*It is better to have a
permanent income than
to be fascinating.*

The Model Millionaire

*We in the House of Lords
are never in touch with
public opinion. That makes
us a civilised body.*

Lord Illingworth, *A Woman of No Importance*

The only way to atone for being occasionally a little overdressed is by being always absolutely overeducated.

Phrases and Philosophies for the Use of the Young

*After the first glass you see
things as you wish they were.
After the second glass you
see things as they are not.
Finally, you see things as they
really are, and that is the most
horrible thing in the world.*

On absinthe

*There is always
more brass than brains
in an aristocracy.*

Prince Paul, *Vera; or, The Nihilists*

*Hard work is simply the
refuge of people who have
nothing whatever to do.*

'The Remarkable Rocket'

In this world there are only two tragedies. One is not getting what one wants, and the other is getting it.

Mr Dumby, *Lady Windermere's Fan*

*I am always astonishing
myself. It is the only thing
that makes life worth living.*

Lord Illingworth, *A Woman of No Importance*

*The only thing that can
console one for being poor
is extravagance. The only
thing that can console one
for being rich is economy.*

A Few Maxims for the Instruction of the Over-Educated

Time is a waste of money.

Phrases and Philosophies for the Use of the Young

*We are specially
designed to appeal to
the sense of humour.*

De Profundis

*He was always late on
principle, his principle
being that punctuality
is the thief of time.*

The Picture of Dorian Gray

Art and Aesthetics

Consistency is the last refuge of the unimaginative.

'The Relation of Dress to Art'

Art is the only serious thing in the world. And the artist is the only person who is never serious.

A Few Maxims for the Instruction of the Over-Educated

The more we study Art, the less we care for Nature.

Vivian, 'The Decay of Lying'

*There is much to be said
in favour of modern
journalism. By giving us the
opinions of the uneducated,
it keeps us in touch with the
ignorance of the community.*

Gilbert, *The Critic as Artist*

A poet can survive
everything but a misprint.

The Children of the Poets'

Of course the music is a great difficulty. You see, if one plays good music, people don't listen, and if one plays bad music, people don't talk.

Algernon, *The Importance of Being Earnest*

Only dull people are
brilliant at breakfast.

Mrs Cheveley, An Ideal Husband

Art is the most intense mode of individualism that the world has known.

The Soul of Man Under Socialism

There is no such thing as a moral or an immoral book. Books are well written, or badly written. That is all.

Preface, *The Picture of Dorian Gray*

Anybody can make history. Only a great man can write it.

Gilbert, *The Critic as Artist*

I put all my genius into my life; I put only my talent into my works.

It is absurd to have a hard-and-fast rule about what one should read and what one shouldn't. More than half of modern culture depends on what one shouldn't read.

Algernon, *The Importance of Being Earnest*

Psychology is in its infancy, as a science. I hope, in the interests of Art, it will always remain so.

All art is immoral.

Gilbert, *The Critic as Artist*

*If Nature had been
comfortable, mankind
would never have
invented architecture.*

Vivian, 'The Decay of Lying'

The work of art is to dominate the spectator: the spectator is not to dominate the work of art.

The Soul of Man Under Socialism

*Action... is the last
resource of those who
know not how to dream.*

Gilbert, *The Critic as Artist*

Art finds her own perfection within, and not outside of herself. She is not to be judged by any external standard of resemblance. She is a veil, rather than a mirror.

Vivian, 'The Decay of Lying'

Lady Hunstanton: *But
do you believe all that is
written in the newspapers?*
Lord Illingworth: *I do.
Nowadays it is only the
unreadable that occurs.*

A Woman of No Importance

Musical people are so absurdly unreasonable. They always want one to be perfectly dumb at the very moment when one is longing to be absolutely deaf.

Mabel Chiltern, *An Ideal Husband*

In old days books were written by men of letters and read by the public. Nowadays books are written by the public and read by nobody.

A Few Maxims for the Instruction of the Over-Educated

*Oh! journalism is
unreadable, and
literature is not read.*

Gilbert, *The Critic as Artist*

*People sometimes inquire
what form of government is
most suitable for an artist to
live under. To this question
there is only one answer. The
form of government that is
most suitable to the artist
is no government at all.*

The Soul of Man Under Socialism

The only artists I have ever known who are personally delightful are bad artists.

Lord Henry, *The Picture of Dorian Gray*

One's Family

*I can't help detesting
my relations. I suppose
it comes from the fact
that none of us can stand
other people having the
same faults as ourselves.*

Lord Henry, *The Picture of Dorian Gray*

Mothers, of course, are all right. They pay a chap's bills and don't bother him. But fathers bother a chap and never pay his bills.

Jack, *The Importance of Being Earnest*

Fathers should be neither seen nor heard. That is the only proper basis for family life. Mothers are different. Mothers are darlings.

Lord Goring, *An Ideal Husband*

All women become like their mothers. That is their tragedy. No man does. That's his.

Algernon, *The Importance of Being Earnest*

Children begin by loving their parents. After a time they judge them. Rarely, if ever, do they forgive them.

Lord Illingworth, *A Woman of No Importance*

Oh, why will parents always appear at the wrong time? Some extraordinary mistake in nature, I suppose.

Lord Goring, *An Ideal Husband*

Society

There is only one thing in the world worse than being talked about, and that is not being talked about.

Lord Henry, *The Picture of Dorian Gray*

My own business always bores me to death. I prefer other people's.

Cecil Graham, *Lady Windermere's Fan*

Never speak disrespectfully of Society... Only people who can't get into it do that.

Lady Bracknell, *The Importance of Being Earnest*

Fashion is what one wears oneself. What is unfashionable is what other people wear.

Lord Goring, *An Ideal Husband*

No class is ever really
conscious of its own
suffering. They have to
be told of it by other
people, and they often
entirely disbelieve them.

The Soul of Man Under Socialism

*I don't at all like knowing
what people say of me
behind my back. It makes
me far too conceited.*

Lord Goring, *An Ideal Husband*

Gossip is charming!
History is merely gossip.
But scandal is gossip made
tedious by morality.

Cecil Graham, *Lady Windermere's Fan*

When one pays a visit
it is for the purpose of
wasting other people's
time, not one's own.

Lord Goring, *An Ideal Husband*

And, after all, what is a fashion? From the artistic point of view, it is usually a form of ugliness so intolerable that we have to alter it every six months.

'The Philosophy of Dress'

*In the old days men
had the rack. Now
they have the press.*

The Soul of Man Under Socialism

Gerald: *I suppose society
is wonderfully delightful!*
Lord Illingworth: *To be in it
is merely a bore. But to be
out of it simply a tragedy.*

A Woman of No Importance

I am the only person in the world I should like to know thoroughly.

Mr Dumby, *Lady Windermere's Fan*

Wilde's Wisdom

The only thing that one really knows about human nature is that it changes. Change is the one quality we can predicate of it.

The Soul of Man Under Socialism

It is a very sad thing that nowadays there is so little useless information.

A Few Maxims for the Instruction of the Over-Educated

Most people are other people. Their thoughts are someone else's opinions, their lives a mimicry, their passions a quotation.

De Profundis

People who count their chickens before they are hatched act very wisely because chickens run about so absurdly that it's impossible to count them accurately.

Letter from Paris, May 1900

To be great is to be misunderstood.

Letter to James McNeill Whistler

*The old believe everything;
the middle-aged suspect
everything; the young
know everything.*

Phrases and Philosophies for the Use of the Young

A little sincerity is a dangerous thing, and a great deal of it is absolutely fatal.

Gilbert, *The Critic as Artist*

If you're interested in finding
out more about our books,
find us on Facebook at
Summersdale Publishers and follow
us on Twitter at @Summersdale.

www.summersdale.com